TIME ZONE MAP

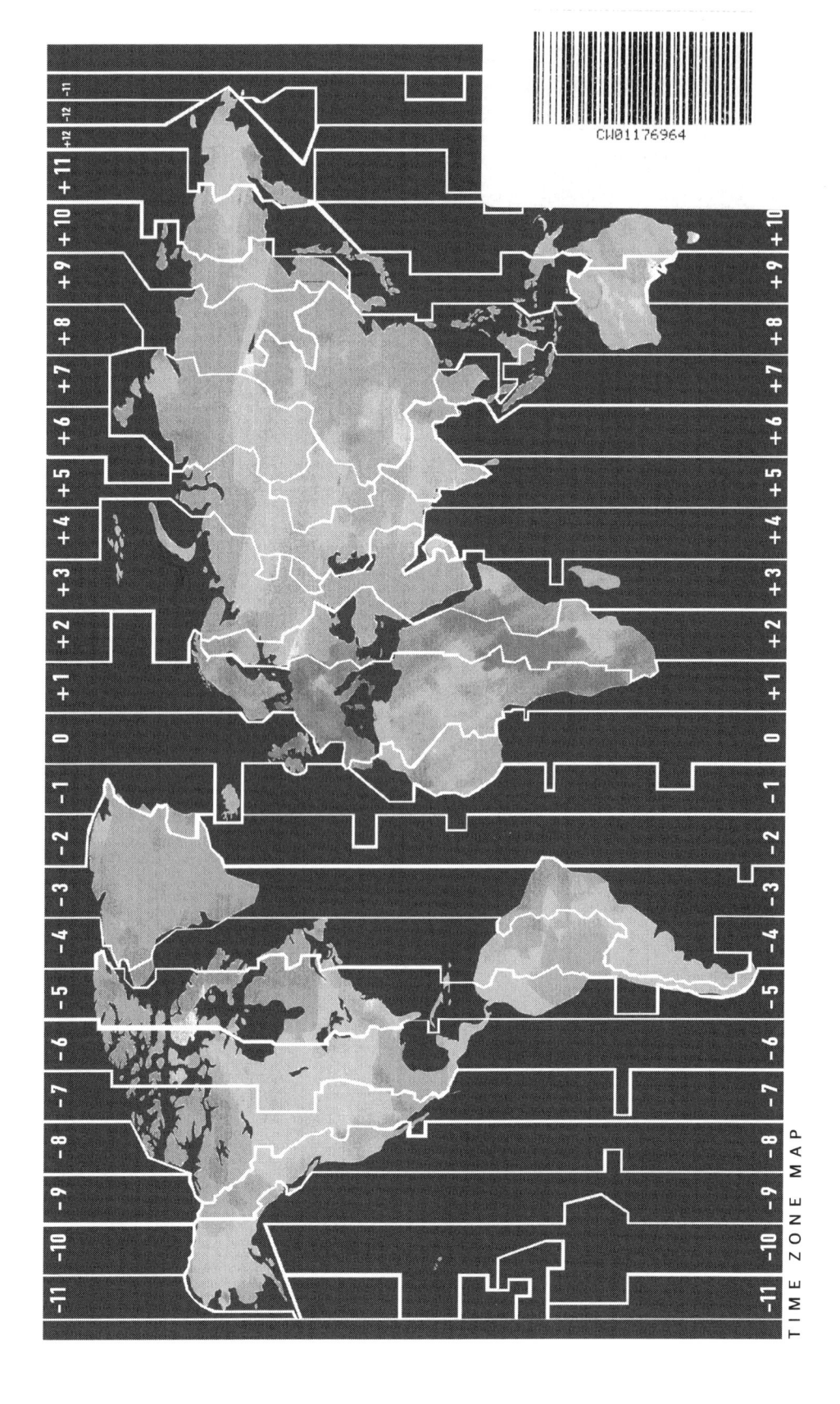

DESTINATION(S):

GOOD TO KNOW ABOUT REGION AND CULTURE:

PACKING LIST

TO DO BEFORE LEAVING

BUCKET LIST

BUDGET

TOTAL:

TOTAL:

LOCATION: DATE:

LOCATION: DATE:

LOCATION: DATE:

LOCATION: DATE:

LOCATION: DATE:

LOCATION: DATE:

LOCATION: DATE:

LOCATION: DATE:

LOCATION: DATE:

LOCATION: DATE:

LOCATION: DATE:

LOCATION: DATE:

LOCATION: DATE:

LOCATION: DATE:

LOCATION: DATE:

LOCATION: DATE:

LOCATION: DATE:

LOCATION: DATE:

LOCATION: DATE:

LOCATION: DATE:

LOCATION: DATE:

LOCATION: DATE:

LOCATION: DATE:

LOCATION: DATE:

LOCATION: DATE:

LOCATION: DATE:

LOCATION: DATE:

LOCATION: DATE:

LOCATION: DATE:

LOCATION: DATE:

LOCATION: DATE:

LOCATION: DATE:

LOCATION: DATE:

LOCATION: DATE:

LOCATION: DATE:

LOCATION: DATE:

LOCATION: DATE:

LOCATION: DATE:

LOCATION: DATE:

LOCATION: DATE:

LOCATION: DATE:

LOCATION: DATE:

LOCATION: DATE:

LOCATION: DATE:

LOCATION: DATE:

LOCATION: DATE:

LOCATION: DATE:

LOCATION: DATE:

LOCATION: DATE:

LOCATION: DATE:

LOCATION: DATE:

LOCATION: DATE:

LOCATION: DATE:

DESTINATION(S):

GOOD TO KNOW ABOUT REGION AND CULTURE:

PACKING LIST

TO DO BEFORE LEAVING

BUCKET LIST

BUDGET

TOTAL:

TOTAL:

LOCATION: DATE:

LOCATION: DATE:

LOCATION: DATE:

LOCATION: DATE:

LOCATION: DATE:

LOCATION: DATE:

LOCATION: DATE:

LOCATION: DATE:

LOCATION: DATE:

LOCATION: DATE:

LOCATION: DATE:

LOCATION: DATE:

LOCATION: DATE:

LOCATION: DATE:

LOCATION: DATE:

LOCATION: DATE:

LOCATION: DATE:

LOCATION: DATE:

LOCATION: DATE:

LOCATION: DATE:

LOCATION: DATE:

LOCATION: DATE:

LOCATION: DATE:

LOCATION: DATE:

LOCATION: DATE:

LOCATION: DATE:

LOCATION: DATE:

LOCATION: DATE:

LOCATION: DATE:

LOCATION: DATE:

LOCATION: DATE:

LOCATION: DATE:

LOCATION: DATE:

LOCATION: DATE:

LOCATION: DATE:

LOCATION: DATE:

LOCATION: DATE:

LOCATION: DATE:

LOCATION: DATE:

LOCATION: DATE:

LOCATION: DATE:

LOCATION: DATE:

LOCATION: DATE:

LOCATION: DATE:

LOCATION: DATE:

LOCATION: DATE:

LOCATION: DATE:

LOCATION: DATE:

LOCATION: DATE:

LOCATION: DATE:

Printed in Great Britain
by Amazon